570

D1283720

ABOUT # APPLES

FROM ORCHARD TO MARKET

By Mary Moore Green

Illustrated by Henry Luhrs

Melmont Publishers, Inc.
Chicago, Illinois

Dedicated to the memory of Grandfather
Arthur R. Green who planted the apple
orchards on the Green farm and who loved
and respected children, grown-ups, and
trees. Dedicated also to Grandfather Green's
grandchildren who live on and love the
apple farm.

Library of Congress Catalog Card Number 60-5161

ABOUT **APPLES**

FROM ORCHARD TO MARKET

The Green family has lived in Michigan since 1832. Davy Crockett was alive when President Andrew Jackson signed the grant that gave the land to Great-grandfather Green.

Great-grandfather Green worked hard to make a clearing in the thick forest for his home and for his fields.

The apple orchard was started about fifty years later by the son of Great-grandfather Green.

Grandfather Green chose the site for the apple orchard. It was a gently rolling hillside. Here the late frosts of the cool Michigan springtime would be less likely to harm the budding trees.

The orchard was planted in the spring of the year. The sandy hillside was ploughed and cultivated. Then the holes for the young trees were dug.

Grandfather Green bought trees that were two or three years old from a nursery. He planted them about thirty-six feet apart so they would have plenty of room in which to grow.

Not many of Grandfather Green's trees died the next winter. When spring came around again, he replaced those that had.

Farmer Green is the son of Grandfather Green. He now lives on the farm with his wife and their three boys—George, Jimmy, and Robert. Farmer Green raises apples as his father did. George, the oldest boy, helps him.

During January and February, Farmer Green and George prune the apple trees. They cut away small branches that spoil the shape of a tree. They cut away dead branches that keep out the sun.

George prunes the lower branches. He uses a tree saw and pruning shears.

Farmer Green prunes the upper branches. He stands on his homemade squirrel. This is a platform that can be raised as high as fourteen feet. It is put onto the front of the tractor.

After the pruning, the branches must be cleared away. Farmer Green uses his homemade buckrake for this.

The buckrake is a big wooden fork put onto the front of the tractor. It pushes the branches into a pile at the end of each row of trees.

George sets fire to the piles. Jimmy and
Robert call this the apple fire. They watch
but they are very careful. They stand far
back from the blaze.

Spring is spraying time on the Green
farm. The first spray is put on just before
the green tips of the leaves begin to show.
The trees are sprayed several times between
blossom time and harvest time.

Farmer Green uses a chemical spray.
Insects and disease must not be allowed
to hurt the new leaves and the fruit
later on.

Early each spring, Farmer Green also puts
fertilizer on his orchard. It is spread around
the trees just under their outer branches.
The spring rains carry this food down to the
roots of the trees.

Later in spring, Farmer Green's orchard
is pink and white. The boys walk up the
gentle slopes between the trees. "How
beautiful!" they say. "How beautiful!" The
wind blows. Petals fall like snow. "How
beautiful!"

Spring is a busy time for the honey-bees. From morning until night they gather the nectar from the apple blossoms. Bzzzzz! The air is filled with humming.

Farmer Green knows the bees help his trees bear fruit. They carry the golden pollen on their furry legs, from one apple blossom to another. This fine yellow dust makes an apple grow where once there was only a blossom.

After blossom time is over, Farmer Green sprays a fertilizer on the trees. The leaves absorb it. It feeds the trees more quickly than fertilizer spread on the ground.

In early summer the little apples appear. Some fall from the trees when they are still quite young. Farmer Green calls this the June drop. It does not worry him. He knows if a tree bears too many apples they may not all grow big enough to sell.

Farmer Green may use a spray that will thin out the apples on the trees. Sometimes he and George pick the little apples by hand. Those left on the trees are spaced eight to ten inches apart. This gives each apple a chance to grow large.

If the season is a dry one, Farmer Green irrigates his orchard several times during the summer. He uses a large tank mounted on an old truck. He gives each tree 250 gallons of water each time he waters it.

An irrigation system would make Farmer Green's work easier. Then there would be pipes between the rows of trees. Water would spray through the many small holes in the pipes. But this kind of irrigation would cost a great deal. That is why Farmer Green uses the tank on the truck.

At last it is time to pick the apples. Farmer Green belongs to the Southeastern Michigan Growers Association. It sends him pickers at harvest time.

Farmer Green's pickers usually come from the island of Jamaica. They live on the farm during apple picking season.

Farmer Green begins to harvest the early apples — Dutchess, Astrachan, and Transparent—about the middle of August. He harvests the Wealthys, Jonathans, McIntoshes, Spys, Steel Reds, and Delicious through September and October.

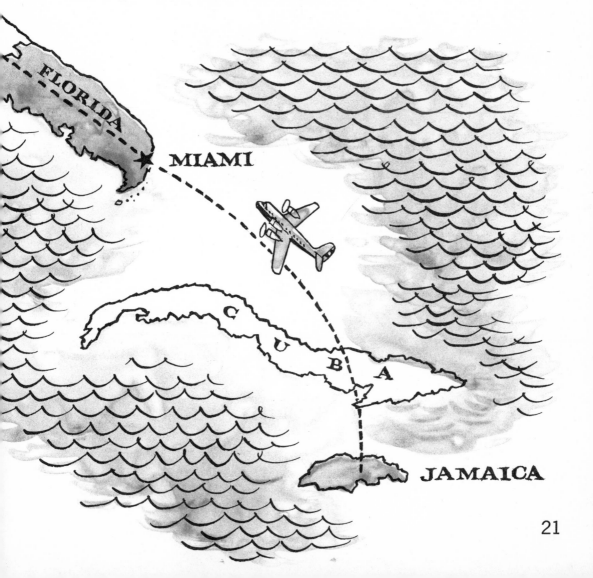

Crates to hold the apples are put in the orchard. The pickers pick the apples into bags hung over their shoulders. When a bag is full, the picker puts the apples into a crate. He must be careful not to bruise them.

The crates of apples are put onto wagons and taken to the apple storage.

The storage is a building in which Farmer Green keeps his apples until they are sold. It will hold 8,000 bushels of apples. A refrigeration plant keeps the apples at just the right temperature.

Load after load is brought in. At last the men finish the picking. The storage is filled with the red, yellow, and green fruit. The air inside the storage is filled with the sweet tangy odor of crisp, firm apples.

The crates are put on wooden cross pieces laid on the floor. They are stacked ten crates high. A fork lift on the front of the tractor helps move the crates from place to place.

During the winter Farmer Green floods the floor of his storage with water. This keeps the air moist. The moist air keeps the apples firm and crisp.

Farmer Green uses a conveyor belt to take the crates of apples into the sorting room. Here the apples are passed over a belt that drops out the small apples. They will be used for cider.

The rest of the apples are carried along over rollers covered with cloth. The rollers polish the apples and wipe off any spray that may have been left on them.

Next, the apples move along a belt. They fall into bins through different sized openings in the belt. The bins are padded to keep the apples from being bruised. Any apples that are bruised are used for cider.

As the apples are graded according to size they are packed into crates. Each crate has a liner that protects the apples from bruises, dust, and dirt.

The sale of apples goes on the year round on the Green farm. Farmer Green's truck takes many loads of apples to the Detroit Eastern Market. Farmer Green also sells apples to supermarkets in and around Detroit. He has a roadside stand in front of his house. Growing and selling apples is Farmer Green's way of making a living.

Farmer Green does not sell cider. He has only a small hand press which he uses to make cider for his own family.

"Cider is better than pop," say the Green boys as they drink tall glasses of the cold amber juice. "Cider is the best drink of all."

Winter comes. The apple trees are bare. Long winter evenings call for popcorn and apples or cider.

There is always a bowl of apples on the table in the Green living room. Farmer Green and his family eat apples while they read or watch television.

Mother Green bakes apple pies and cooks apple sauce for the family.

Soon spring will be here. The orchards will bloom again.

Mary Moore Green was born on a farm near Romulus, Michigan. She holds a Bachelor of Science degree from Eastern Michigan University at Ypsilanti.

Mrs. Green has taught all of the elementary grades, from kindergarten through sixth, in various Michigan schools. At present she is a consultant to elementary teachers in the Pontiac school system.

Mrs. Green, her husband, and their three sons live on the apple farm that has been in the family for over 100 years. Mr. Green has been in the apple growing business for the past twenty-five years.

Henry Luhrs, a Californian by birth, actually has not spent too much time in his native state. His work as a free lance illustrator has taken him both to New York and Chicago.

Mr. Luhrs' illustrations have appeared in such magazines as **Cosmopolitan, Colliers,** and **Red Book**. He has also illustrated a number of children's books for the Whitman Publishing Company of Racine, Wisconsin.

Mr. Luhrs received his art training at the California Institute of Art in San Francisco, as well as the Art League and Grand Central Art School in New York. At present, he and Mrs. Luhrs make their home in Laguna Beach, California.